I0007137

Make-Money-Online Series

How to Make Money
Writing for the Internet

A Step-by-Step Guide
to Publishing Your Work Online

Blake Webster

Steve Boga

To aspiring writers everywhere.

Books by Blake Webster & Steve Boga

How to Self-Publish Your Book the CreateSpace Way

How to Start Your Online Photography Store

Greener Living Today: Forty Ways to a Greener Lifestyle

How to Umpire Baseball and Softball: An Introduction to Basic Umpire Skills

You Be the Judge: An Introduction to Basic Umpiring Skills (DVD)

The Humorous Side of Major League Baseball: An Umpire's Look Back at Bizarre Plays, Brawls, Ejections, Funny Stories, Knotty Problems, Tough Calls and More

Fountain of Youth: Refresh Your Life at Any Age with 60 Minutes of Play a Day

How to Start Your Online Affiliate Store: Step-by-Step Guide to Making Money Online

Environmentalists in Action: Profiles of Green Pioneers

Contents

Introduction

Let's start with this: The world needs writers more than ever. Text—and increasingly online text—is still our strongest communication tool. Of course, words communicate much more than their literal meaning.

Your online text should perform multiple tasks. Ideally it should:

- Offer benefit

- Present an image

- Set a tone

- Entertain

- Appeal to search engines

- Draw traffic

- Generate links

- Promote or market

Set Yourself Apart

With the rise of the Internet and the fall of the economy, aspiring writers face formidable competition. If you want to generate income writing online content, you must stand out from the crowd.

You might start here:

- Pay attention to keywords in titles and headings.

- Answer the reader's question, "What's in it for me?" in the lead.

- Develop a distinctive voice in the first-person.

- Write about a variety of topics . . . and become an expert in one or more. Develop a niche.

- Do the research; use facts in your writing and quote reputable sources.

- Eliminate spelling and grammar errors, which shred your credibility and can cause an otherwise quality article to be rejected.

- Consider your name and writing as a label or brand. Keep the same username across sites to help you expand that brand.

- Learn how to write about sensitive or controversial topics.

- Keep it short and simple (KISS). No wasted words.

- Include a call to action (sign up, join, visit me).

- Slow the reader's eye with speed bumps. Break up large blocks of text. Use bullets for easier reading, and caps and/or boldface to make subtitles pop out. Whitespace, too, gives the eye a break.

- Anticipate your readers' questions and provide the details necessary to answer them. Don't make them search elsewhere.

- Be aware of your online presence. When you post in forums, they come up in searches. Tone down wild accusations. A potential employer may be reading.

Now, are you ready to take up the challenge of writing online?

Know Your Online Audience

Online vs Print Writing

Before you write for the Internet, you must first understand the basic differences between print and online content. As Internet Business Strategist Garth Buchholz says, "One involves reading paper, the other involves reading light." But the differences go beyond that.

Online content is not just about words. Much more than print media, it involves presentation and interaction; layout and design are especially critical in a visual medium like the Web. Analyze the online environment in which your content will appear. After all, if you were writing a television commercial, you wouldn't simply compose text without knowing what audiovisuals will accompany it.

Consider the following when writing for an online audience:

▪ Words are graphical images, too. We tend to notice font style, color, size, and how the text appears as a visual block even before we begin to extract meaning.

▪ Identify your audience early on. As with any medium, you must know your "community" of readers/listeners/viewers. First, determine your purpose. Is it pedagogical? Promotional? Are you creating content for an Internet site? An email newsletter? What are your readers' interests? Education? Age range? Biases?

- Make sure your online content can be easily scanned. Most Internet readers have a search-and-retrieve mentality and lack the patience necessary to read large blocks of narrative text. When creating web text, make sure it's chunked out—that is, broken into smaller blocks of text separated by subheadings, bullets, and white space.

- Write strong titles, headings, and subheadings (meta-content). Many of your readers will want to scan for the keywords or links they need, while bypassing the rest. Good subheadings also help the reader understand the navigation and organization of the content. If we read only the headings and subheadings of your article, we should have a good idea of what it's about.

- Make good use of links. Your copy can probably be trimmed if you simply link to other webpages that offer the same information. Moreover, readers like to interact on the Web, and links help them do that.

- Make your readers want to read on. Use no unnecessary verbiage, favor the active voice, and follow the rules of grammar. When appropriate, take a stand. Give your writing attitude, but avoid sounding pretentious or arrogant.

- Use the "inverted pyramid" structure of writing favored by journalists. To catch the reader's attention, make sure your five W's (*who, what, when, where, why*) and also how are near the top. Details of lesser importance should follow from general to specific (the inverted pyramid). Thus, if we read only the first few lines, we should have a good idea of the main points in the article.

- Avoid simply repurposing documents for the Web. Repurposing occurs when you grab a document created for print and attach it to a website. While sometimes necessary, it's the laziest, least-effective way to put content on the Internet. Instead, consider how the content can be rewritten, redesigned, and laid out for maximum reader impact in the online environment.

Get to Know the New Reader

As media theorist Marshall McLuhan pointed out in the 1960s, media are not just passive channels of information—they shape the way we think. Clearly, the Internet has had an enormous impact on human thinking. But good or bad?

Some believe the Net is chipping away at our capacity for concentration and contemplation. Increasingly, our minds expect to take in information the way the Net distributes it: in a swiftly moving stream of particles.

Thanks to the explosion of online text and text-messaging, we may be reading more today than we did forty years ago, when television was our medium of choice. But it's a different kind of reading, prompting a different kind of thinking. "We are not only *what* we read," says Maryanne Wolf, a developmental psychologist at Tufts University and author of *Proust and the Squid: The Story and Science of the Reading Brain*. "We are *how* we read."

The Internet, which elevates efficiency and immediacy above all else, may be weakening our capacity for the kind of deep reading that emerged in the fifteenth century with the printing press, and which created readers for longer works of prose. When we read online, Wolf says, we tend to become "mere decoders of information." In other words, we risk losing our ability to interpret text, to forge the rich mental connections we make when we read deeply and without distraction.

For distraction is everywhere on the Internet: hyperlinks, blinking ads, and other digital bells and whistles. While you're reading the *Wall Street Journal* online, you might hear a beep and see a box announcing a new email message. The result is to scatter our attention and shatter our concentration.

Nicholas Carr in his piece for *The Atlantic*, "Is Google Making us Stupid?" laments his changing brain:

Over the past few years I've had an uncomfortable sense that someone, or something, has been tinkering with my brain, remapping the neural circuitry, reprogramming the memory. My mind isn't going—so far as I can tell—but it's changing. I'm not thinking the way I used to think. I can feel it most strongly when I'm reading. Immersing myself in a book or a lengthy article used to be easy. My mind would get caught up in the narrative or the turns of the argument, and I'd spend hours strolling through long stretches of prose. That's rarely the case anymore. Now my concentration often starts to drift after two or three pages. I get fidgety, lose the thread, begin looking for something else to do. I feel as if I'm always dragging my wayward brain back to the text. The deep reading that used to come naturally has become a struggle.

Write for Search Engines

Learn SEO

A sound understanding of search-engine optimization (SEO) is vital for anyone hoping to succeed as an Internet writer.

SEO is the process of improving the visibility of a website or webpage in search engines via unpaid ("organic" or "algorithmic") search results. In general, the higher on the page and the more frequently a site appears in a search-results list, the more visitors it will receive from the search engine.

In print media, a writer's work is included in a bound publication that already has a captive audience. In contrast, each online article stands alone and must be optimized for search engines in order to attract any readers at all. Each article must contain specific cues about its purpose. That means stitching together keywords—and in a way that appears effortless and natural.

Put another way, SEO writing is creating content that includes keywords and phrases to help search engines—and thus readers—find a specific article.

Mix in Keywords

You should place appropriate keywords throughout your site, in your titles, text, URLs, and image names.

According to *PC World*, the title tag and page header are the most important placements. Think of your keywords as search terms—how would someone looking for information on this topic search for it?

Be judicious in your keyword use. Cramming dozens of keywords into your text will get you labeled a spammer, and search-engine spiders are programmed to ignore sites guilty of "keyword-stuffing."

Achieve Scanability

Besides including the right keywords, your SEO content must be scanned easily. Web readers want to find the information they need quickly, often without reading an entire article. For optimum scanning, SEO articles should:

- Be broken into chunks.

- Have keyword-rich subheadings.

- Have short paragraphs, no more than 50-75 words.

- Give information in bulleted or numbered lists.

Add Links

Integrating internal links into your site is an easy way to boost traffic to individual pages. As with all other SEO approaches, be sure your links are appropriate and not excessive, lest you annoy your visitors.

Routinely link back to your archives when creating new content.

Add Captions to Your Images

Because spiders do not search the text inside your images, it's important to add captions to all your pictures. Make the words associated with your images as descriptive and keyword-rich as possible.

Start with your image names. Adding an ALT tag allows you to include a keyword-rich description for every image on your site.

Update Frequently

Your content needs to be fresh. Frequent updating is crucial for boosting traffic. The most search-engine-friendly sites are full of oft-updated, useful information about a specific service, product, topic, or discipline.

Mix in a Blog

One way to ensure new content is to integrate a blog. A blog allows you to a) reach out to your readers, b) create more opportunities for internal and external linking, and c) give your site a more personal voice.

Create and Promote a Website

Want to increase exposure to your books, articles, and editorial services? Create a website. Once your site is up, search-engine optimization (SEO) will play a key role in determining its success. Remember, no matter how attractive your new site, it will serve no purpose if it's not seen.

If you've written a book and made good use of keywords in your title, part of the battle for search positioning has already been won. Google loves Amazon content and spiders the site constantly.

The title of your book should become the title of the book's product page. Keywords wisely used in title tags are one of the best SEO practices available.

Thanks in part to the keywords in our title tags, our book, *How to Start Your Online Affiliate Store*, does especially well with certain searches. For example, when you type the search query "how to start your online affiliate store," our Amazon product page shows up second out of almost twenty million results. Change one word—"how to start an online affiliate store"—and we rank eighth. The results are similar at Yahoo.

Another bonus: Affiliate sites that carry the Amazon feed for a book title tend to turn up higher in search results based on that book's title. And CreateSpace eStore listings tend to show up higher in search results than other sites because of their affiliation with Amazon.

We want to apply the same concepts when setting up our promotional website. Make good use of title keywords in the domain name and the title pages of your site.

Design a Website

An excellent way to promote your writing is to develop a website devoted to providing information about it.

Here are some basic guidelines for getting started.

1. Register Your Domain Name

First, you need to register a domain name. We recommend choosing a domain name that contains keywords pertaining to your title.

For example:

www.makemoneyonlineseries.com
www.howtoumpirebaseball.com

We register all of our domains with GoDaddy, one of the largest registrars, but you can use any registrar you feel comfortable with, such as HostGator or Network Solutions.

2. Find a Hosting Provider

Once you've registered your domain, you need to set it up with a hosting provider. If you have a GoDaddy account, you can use GoDaddy as the provider.

We prefer to use hosting companies that provide *cPanel*, a control panel for the back-end administration of our domains and sites. GoDaddy is fine, but it can be a little slow and cumbersome when it comes to setting up email accounts and *MySql databases*, a relational database-management system.

We believe HostGator is the best for site setup. A large provider out of Texas, HostGator offers top-notch support, good backup, and a server system that responds quickly to setup procedures.

After choosing your provider, you must change the *name server information* so that the domain points to your new hosting service. If you are using hosting from the same company with which you registered the domain, you probably won't have to change this. Check with the hosting company's technical support.

Name server information will look something like this:

NS1.1111.HOSTGATOR.COM and
NS2.1112.HOSTGATOR.COM

After setting up a hosting account, you will usually be provided with the name server information by email, along with setup instructions.

3. Select a Web Platform

We recommend using WordPress as a content-management system for most sites.

WordPress, an open-source blog-publishing platform powered by PHP and MySQL, can be used for basic content management. It includes many features, including a user-friendly administration panel, a rich plug-in architecture, and an advanced templating system.

Hosting companies offering cPanel will provide you with a "wizard" for setting up WordPress on your new site. Again, HostGator offers excellent technical support if you run into any WordPress installation problems.

When installing WordPress, you will be asked the name of your site. This is where you add the title of your book. It will appear in the title of all your post pages and boost your search-engine positioning.

You can learn more about working with WordPress by visiting www.wordpress.org.

4. Design a Theme/Template

The next step in your setup is to choose and upload a design for your site.

WordPress is compatible with a variety of themes that will enhance the look and design of your site. Although thousands of themes are free, we tend to gravitate toward higher-quality themes, usually costing $25 to $75. It's your choice. Higher-quality themes are usually better optimized for search engines thanks to good use of title and header tags (<h1> to <h6> tags are used to define HTML headings), but all WordPress coding is clean and favored by search engines.

To learn more about themes and free downloads, visit the WordPress site at www.wordpress.org.

5. Lay Out the Content

We follow a basic formula when organizing and laying out content for a site. It consists of creating five posts that contain information about different aspects of the product or service. You can create more posts, but five is enough for now. In the examples below, the product is a book.

Post One: *Title*. Besides the title and subtitle, include a description of your book. It need not be long.

Post Two: *Preface*. This can be the same as the book's Preface, though if it's quite long, you might want to pull an excerpt. Regardless, don't give away too much of the book's main content.

Post Three: *Author Bio*. Sell yourself, but not ostentatiously.

Post Four: *Excerpt* from the book. We usually insert an excerpt from the first chapter, but you can use any content you believe showcases the quality of the book.

Post Five: *Buy Now*. Include information about the price of the book, along with a link to the Amazon product page.

Get Your Site Indexed Using Backlinks and Pings

Now you want to get your site indexed in Google. Because we use WordPress, we often find our new sites spidered and indexed in Google within twenty-four hours. This is greatly due to the pinging services that WordPress notifies.

Pinging

Update services—Pings—are tools that let other people know you've updated your blog. WordPress automatically notifies popular update services, such as Ping-o-Matic, that you've updated your blog by sending a ping each time you create or change a post. Update services process the ping and add your site's update to their databases. The title of your new version and an excerpt will appear in the update, along with a link back to the post's web address.

Ping lists can be added from your WordPress dashboard. In the left navigation column, select "Settings/Writing." At the bottom of the Writing page look for a field labeled "Update Services." Paste in your list of ping services, and click on the button labeled "Save Changes."

You can obtain a comprehensive Ping list at: www.prelovac.com/vladimir/wordpress-ping-list.

Backlinking

In addition to Pings, you will want to obtain backlinks from other sites, for indexing purposes and to improve Pagerank. Here are two suggestions for effective back-linking:

1. If you have any preexisting sites, or know people who have sites that have age, page rank, or are regularly spidered by the search engines, add a link to your new site.

2. We have a subscription with USFreeads (www.usfreeads.com), and after we set up a new site, we place a classified ad there that contains a link back to the new site. Our ad contains only the title of the site, a description, a price tag of zero, and the web address. Google spiders USFreeads on the hour, so you will see your ad indexed in Google immediately. The Google spider will then follow the link to your site.

RSS Feeds

Another great feature of WordPress is that it produces *RSS* (Real Simple Syndication) feeds of the content on your site. There are hundreds of RSS feed directories, and other websites will pull the feeds from these directories and display the feed content on their own sites. The feeds contain a link back to the source of the feed, thus provid-ing you with potential traffic and another backlink to your site.

We use a program called Traffic Mania RSS Bot, which submits our feeds to about 40 RSS feed directories. You can find out more about RSS Bot at www.incansoft.com.

It will help the online promotion of your new site if you build backlinks on a regular basis; however, if you find that you are building backlinks haphazardly, or not at all, consider outsourcing your SEO campaign to a certified SEO consultant.

Find more tips on backlinking and promoting your site at Basic SEO Direct, www.basicseodirect.com.

AdWords

Another way to promote your writings is to make use of Google Adwords. AdWords is Google's flagship advertising product and main source of revenue. AdWords offers pay-per-click (PPC) advertising for both text and banner ads. Google's text ads are short, consisting of one title line and two content text lines.

AdWords can be pricey because advertisers bid for ad placement. If your subject is a highly competitive one—say, weight loss or cosmetic surgery—you may want to avoid this approach. On the other hand, if you face little competition, you may be able to purchase advertising for as little as five cents per click.

Make sure the ad's "click thru" URL points to the Amazon product page for your new book.

You can learn more about creating an AdWords account and implementing your advertising campaign by visiting AdWords at http://adwords.google.com.

Social Bookmarking Sites

We find backlinking through social bookmarking sites to be a powerful method for obtaining high Pagerank and search positioning. Social bookmarking is a way for Internet users to share, organize, search, and manage bookmarks of web resources. Unlike file sharing, the resources themselves aren't shared, merely bookmarks that reference them. Social bookmarking helps search engines find and rank content through links. Backlinking through these sites will help promote traffic to your site, contribute to your link-building campaign, and increase your search-engine rankings.

It may be worth your while to spend a few dollars and obtain thousands of legitimate backlinks. We use a company that provides backlinking through a network of over 350 social-bookmarking sites spread over four continents. The process requires submitting your site's RSS feeds to the bookmarking sites. This is yet another benefit of using WordPress, which automatically generates RSS feeds and updates them every time you add new content.

You can find out more about backlinking to social bookmarking sites at Basic SEO Direct, www.basicseodirect.com.

Press Releases

Many people don't appreciate the value of press releases, but it's a method Blake often uses to promote his sites. You can pay as much as $100 for a press release at PRWeb, or you can access the many free press-release sites.

To submit to free press-release sites, we use a program called Traffic Mania Press Bot. It provides a template for compiling your press release so that it conforms to standard press-release protocol.

You can find more information about Press Bot here: http://www.incansoft.com.

Create In-Content Link Posts

"In content" means the links area is associated with an article—or at least a paragraph of text. In-content backlinks carry more weight with search engines than does a single line of text.

Linkvana

SEO companies are constantly looking for writers to develop articles and blog posts that are keyword rich and contain keyword anchor text to be linked back to a client's site. Their writers create short articles—usually 100-200 words—that they submit to services such as Linkvana. Linkvana then posts the articles on its extensive network, thousands of sites that it owns.

Linkvana is a powerful tool for webmasters like Blake, who want to promote their sites, or their clients' sites, for SEO purposes. Start an account with Linkvana, and for $150 per month you gain access to about a thousand sites, all blogs.

Here's the process: You create a blog post of 100-200 words, include a link or two, then add it to the Linkvana queue. Every 24 hrs, the Linkvana system taps into the queue and pulls out the posts that are ready; then a live person reviews the posts, checking for spelling and making sure it contains nothing inappropriate, such as gambling or adult content. Once the post is approved, it goes into a cue for posting.

You can see the power in the Linkvana network, but it is pricey and you do have to write all those posts.

DigitalPoint

DigitalPoint is a webmaster forum and resource center marketplace. It's valuable not just for webmasters but for potential customers. The site is divided into six sections. The Business section contains areas for buying links and selling links.

When Blake uses DigitalPoint, he hunts for customers who want to buy links. More and more, those customers prefer their links embedded in a blog post. Blake, and other companies, often hire writers to produce the content.

For work opportunities, go to the Business section and check out "Writing and Content Development." Other subsections include "Copywriting," "Buy, Sell or Trade/Services/Content Creation," and "Buy, Sell or Trade/Content."

Blog Guest Posts

By forging strategic partnerships with other bloggers, you can a) produce content and put it before the right audience, and b) acquire great content for your own sites.

One type of strategic partnership is called guest posting. The purpose of guest posts is to help both parties grow an audience. To be successful, guest posting must benefit everybody involved.

Here's how it works. A client recently approached Blake for an article on Area Rugs. Blake owns a network of sites in about fifty different categories. Because his interior-design site enjoys high page rank, he was able to charge twenty dollars for a 100-word article on area rugs. He did the research, wrote the post, put it on his site, linked back to the clients' site—all of which took him about twenty minutes.

The Growing Importance of Original Content

Google has long given preference to sites that contain original content, and that's true now more than ever. In February 2011, Google implemented the Panda and Farmer updates to its algorithm. The updates were designed to address the issues of 1) excessive duplicate content and 2) Content Farms, and to remove such sites from the top of Google search results.

Matt Cutts, Google's head of spam, said the update "is designed to reduce rankings for low-quality sites—sites which are low-value add for users, copy content from other websites, or sites that are just not very useful. At the same time, it will provide better rankings for high-quality sites—sites with original content and information such as research, in-depth reports, thoughtful analysis, and so on."

Given these changes to Google's algorithm, it's more important than ever to provide solid, original information to viewers. In this way, writers help businesses maintain their web presence in Google searches.

To learn more about SEO techniques, consider taking one or more of the online courses on search-engine optimization. A good place to start is SEO Certification (searchenginecertification.org). If you take the training and pass the exam, you can receive your certification for as little as $89.

Approach Content Providers

Online content providers offer original SEO content for websites, including SEO press-release content. These companies employ writers to a) edit and ghostwrite their clients' work and/or b) create original content that will be purchased by clients.

When Blake got the idea to develop books for publication on the CreateSpace platform, he decided to put out a book as a test, mostly to see what was required of him regarding layout and graphics. In order to speed the process, he sought help preparing and writing the first book. He found a company called Content Customs (contentcustoms.com).

"A representative immediately contacted me by phone to determine my needs," Blake says. "I'd already prepared the table of contents and written the first two chapters. The rep quoted me a price—about $200. I agreed, and within an hour one of their writers sent me an email asking some questions. In forty-eight hours I had a completed book file to proofread. The writing was solid, and I now had everything I needed to move forward publishing my new book with CreateSpace."

What to Expect from Content Providers

Unless a site says otherwise, you can generally count on the following:

• For tax purposes, you are an independent contractor, not an employee. You are responsible for reporting all income as required by law. The sites below do not withhold income tax from your earnings. If you file federal form 1040, you report such income on Schedule C. The good news: You can deduct any expenses associated with your writing career, including office expenses and mileage. You may even qualify for a home-office deduction.

• Monthly or biweekly payments are sent to you through your PayPal account whenever you accrue a minimum balance of five or ten dollars.

• You can either copy-paste your article or type directly into a field, but it's usually best to compose and edit off-site, then paste it only after you have polished it to a high sheen. Even after you have pasted the article in the field, go through it again with a critical eye. Make sure the text is free of mistakes and that you have proper word count.

• Before you submit an article to a site, study the formatting requirements. Most sites ask you to professionally format your articles in 12 pt. Times New Roman or Arial black font, with single-spaced paragraphs and a double space between paragraphs.

• Sites that demand original material take plagiarism seriously. Plagiarism is the unauthorized use or close imitation of the language and thoughts of another author and the representation of them as one's own original work. If you copy even a sentence or two of another writer's work, it may be plagiarism. And Copyscape is watching [see below].

Spotlight on a Few Content Providers

Bukisa (bukisa.com)

Bukisa offers how-to, informational, and educational content. The site is a self-described "aggregator and a UGC website," providing content in the form of articles, audio/video recordings, and image slideshows.

Bukisa gives its members the opportunity to:

• Share knowledge and get paid for providing quality content.

• Build their own online network of "friends" who can earn money for themselves and for you.

• Boost their exposure on the web and help them build their brand into an online presence.

Major Topics

Automotive, Education, Family, Food/Drinks, Hobbies/Crafts, Home/Garden, Internet, Pets, Relationships, Religion/Spirituality, Reviews, Science/Technology, Self Improvement, Sports/Fitness, Travel.

Costs

Joining and publishing content are free, as are all other functions, such as voting, commenting, and inviting friends to join your network.

Payout

What they say: "Anyone who joins the Bukisa community and shares their knowledge is entitled to a share of the profits."

What they do: Bukisa gives its writers the opportunity to earn a share of the revenue from their content by embedding Google AdSense code within their individual posts. If you do not have an account with Google AdSense, you can open one for free.

Break Studios (breakstudios.com)

What they say: "We are looking for writers who are passionate about their subjects, serious about their writing, and looking to make money writing short, smart pieces in a swift and timely manner . . . If your expertise areas meet with our current topic selection, you'll hear from our assignment desk shortly."

Topics

Break Studios contracts with freelancers to write for its community of "highly popular and humorous" websites, including Break.com, MadeMan, Holy Taco, Cage Potato, Screen Junkies, and Chickipedia.

Once you are approved, you can log in to your personal Dashboard page and browse a list of Titles/Topics. Break Studios will either suggest content assignments that match your skills or you can pick assignments for which you are qualified from the Topics list. You may also suggest your own Titles/Topics to write about. You can find guidelines for suggesting titles at "Submission Guidelines."

Step #1: Claiming an Article

Break Studios provides its writers with dozens of article topics daily. Each topic that matches the areas of expertise you listed on your application will show up on your homepage whenever you log in. Or you can go to the "Claim Content" page and select any topic you like.

For each topic, Break Studios provides the subject, title, subtitle, due date, targeted website, and how much you will be paid after publication.

Step #2: Submitting an Article

When you're ready to submit your completed article for editing, go to the "Article Submission" page and send it. An editor will a) suggest any needed changes or b) accept it as is.

Step #3: Publishing an Article

Once your article is accepted, it gets published to the target website and you will be notified. Articles are generally published within 3-7 days after acceptance. Periodically check the "Made Manual" section of MadeMan.com to see if your articles have been published. At that point, you're free to Blog it, Tweet it, or Facebook it.

Step #4: Getting Paid for an Article

When you sign up, you will provide an email address linked to a PayPal account. Each month, Break Studios will deposit what you are owed into that account.

Break Studios will issue payments on the 1st and 15th of every month. Writers will be paid if they've had articles approved at least four business days before pay date. You either set up a personal account with PayPal or give Break Studios the information for an existing account during signup. Then deposits are made directly into your personal PayPal account.

Payment for articles depends on the nature of the work and the distribution it will receive. You can find the pay rate for each article in the "Content Pool" section of your Break Studios dashboard.

Constant-Content (constant-content.com)

What they say: "Started in 2004 Constant-Content has grown from a small gathering place for writers and publishers, into one of the **Internet's largest marketplaces for content-based SEO business development**. Serving over 10,000 websites by providing them access to almost 30,000 writers, Constant-Content has developed the most comprehensive and quality article production system on the web . . . Built around the fact that top quality original content is the heart and soul of all Search Engine Optimization efforts, all of our articles are subject to **rigorous editorial and plagiarism review**."

Buyers can purchase content through a) an extensive catalogue of existing articles, or b) a custom content request system.

Main Topics

Arts, Culture, Business, General, Health, Lifestyles, Home, Merchandise, Recreation, Regional, Relationships, Science, Society, Sports, Technology.

Other Media

Photography, Illustrations, Video.

Writer Guidelines

Constant-content is looking for professionally written, concise articles free of errors, including sentence-structure, grammar, and punctuation errors. A professionally written article includes an introduction and a conclusion.

Submissions Must Not Include:

- Poetry, fiction, op-eds, or first-person POV.

- Promotional content.

- Active linked web addresses. If you must include web addresses, remove the http://www prefix. Example: Google.com (good), www.google.com (bad).

- Sig lines, bios, or author contact information.

- Plagiarism.

Technical Submission Requirements:

- 12 pt Arial or Times New Roman font.

- A short summary—an original description of the entire article, at least 30 words long.

- A longer summary that includes 1/3 of the article excerpted.

The Process

Once you register at Constant-Content, you will receive almost-daily emails from them that look like this:

You have a new message at Constant-Content

Customer Deter Fuss has requested a new article on Constant-Content; below are the details:

Title: In search of a 1300-word article on conscious eating

Description: I'm searching for a 1300-word article about conscious choices for healthier food, and ways to become a conscious eater.

Number of Articles Needed: 3
Price per Article: $100-150
Length of Article: 1300
Date requested: 2010-12-19 04:02:27

Payout

Constant Content keeps 35 percent of the price of each article and pays the author 65 percent. If you have been referred by another author, the 5 percent commission he or she receives comes out of Constant Content's percentage.

Helium (helium.com)

What they say: "Helium is a knowledge cooperative where our writers are also our editors who read and rate every article on the site. *At Helium, we believe that everyone can contribute what they know to share with millions of readers around the globe* . . . At Helium, great writing rises to the top. And great writing reaps great rewards."

Payout

Helium's payout is based on three factors:

- **Article quality**: The best-written and highest-ranked articles earn the most money. Those ranked at the top will be read more often and are considered more valuable to Helium members, readers, and advertisers.

- **Traffic**: Articles with more page views earn more money.

- **Advertiser interest**: Some topics attract higher-paying advertisers than others. Personal finance will generally draw a higher ad rate than, say, chess.

Once you have reached $25, you can request a payment. Payment is sent via PayPal at the beginning of the following month.

Seed (seed.com)

What they say: "Are you a professional journalist? A world-class expert on a specific topic? Or maybe just someone with a passion and the desire to write about it online? Whether you like to write theater reviews, political essays, tips on building a deck, or opinions about your favorite bands and sports teams, now you can get your words published in a bold new way thanks to AOL. And even better, you can get paid for it."

How? Seed, an open-content submission platform from AOL, wants people to write pieces on current topics. The topics are posted on Seed. When you publish an original piece of work, Seed guarantees that each post you provide will be accessed by others on the extensive AOL Media Network.

Seed assigns, buys, and distributes work for AOL properties, more than eighty websites in all, from Asylum to WoW.com.

Payout

Seed pays its writers in one of two ways:

1. AOL acquires an *exclusive license* to your work for publication on one of its network sites or a third-party site and pays the AOL price (listed with the request).

2. AOL acquires a *limited exclusive license* to your work for publication on one of its network sites and pays you based on the profit it generates (determined by advertising and page views).

Suite 101 (suite101.com)

What they say: "With 13 years online, more than 450,000 articles and over 20,000 professional, paid contract writers, Suite101 is dedicated to delivering great articles by skilled writers. In doing so, we aim to create opportunities for writers at every stage of their careers.

"Suite101's door is open to the curious novice looking for a '101' intro to any of our 3,000 topics, but it's also a meeting place for over 35 million readers each month."

Suite101.com also offers one-on-one editorial coaching, a peer network, and access to comprehensive tutorials on freelance Web writing.

Payout

Rather than receiving a flat fee for each article, writers are paid a share of the revenue earned from a variety of ad sources on Suite 101, including banner ads and Google Adsense ads. Your article earns revenue when a reader a) clicks on an ad, b) views an ad, or c) performs some sort of action related to an ad (such as making a purchase). The rate that each ad pays is determined by the advertiser. Writers who reach 50 articles will receive a 10 percent bonus in revenue share payments.

Textbroker (textbroker.com)

What they say: "Textbroker is your marketplace for unique and exclusive written articles created to your specifications. Our fixed rates make cost planning for projects of all sizes simple. Create multiple orders for website localization and search engine optimization quickly and easily with our unique interface. Whether you need a quick snippet for a website, a well-researched essay, or a sharp press release, our deep database of knowledgeable authors is exactly the right resource to quickly cater to your content needs . . . You don't have to be a professional writer to complete articles; however, the better you write, the more you can earn."

Payout

A writer's income is determined by his or her quality level rating. A higher rating means greater access to orders with higher quality requirements and payment levels. Your work is regularly reviewed and rated by Textbroker's editorial staff. Your quality level is determined by the average rating of your most recent submissions. Thus, you always have the potential to improve your skills, your quality level, and your earnings.

Textbroker writers are paid per word, the amount determined by the client's chosen quality rate. If you are a level 4 author and you choose a level 2 assignment, you will be paid the level 2 rate. The total earnings for each assignment are shown in the Order Detail page.

Price rates:

Quality and payment-rates at Textbroker		
Article Quality	payment per word	payment per 500 words (approximately one letter page)
2 stars: legible	0.7 cents	3.50 USD
3 stars: good quality	1.0 cents	5.00 USD
4 stars: excellent quality	1.4 cents	7.00 USD
5 stars: professional quality	5.0 cents	25.00 USD

Set Your Own Rate

Another option is to set your own prices. Textbroker's
DirectOrder system allows you to set a price for clients
who want to skip the OpenOrder system and send article
requests directly to your inbox. You won't have to search
or compete for assignments, and you can charge the price
you want. The minimum price for DirectOrders starts at
15 cents per word, or $7.50 for 500 words. Textbroker
will add a 30 percent commission to DirectOrders, which
will be included in the client's final price.

Copyscape

Most web publishers want content that is unique. To make sure articles are original and not stolen, check out Copyscape (copyscape.com).

You can use Copyscape to check for plagiarism of your websites, online publications, blogs, marketing materials, or any other online materials. Copyscape offers various levels of protection.

1. **Basic Copyscape**. This service is free. Just enter your web address, and Copyscape will instantly scan the entire Web to check for duplicate content of your pages. Once Copyscape displays the top results for your search, click on a result to see a word-by-word comparison with content on your site. Blocks of text that match the text on your site are highlighted.

2. **Copyscape Premium**. This service costs 5 cents per searched page, but it offers more powerful plagiarism detection. Extra features, such as Batch Search, check for copies of your entire site. Content buyers can use Copyscape Premium to confirm the originality of new content before publishing it online. Site owners can use Copyscape Premium to track down plagiarism of content on their site.

3. **Copysentry**. For a monthly charge, this service provides ongoing protection by automatically monitoring the web for copies of your pages and emailing you whenever new copies are found.

Copysentry Standard offers weekly protection:

- Your pages are checked every week.

- Cost is $4.95/month for up to 10 pages.

- $0.25/month for each additional page.

Copysentry Premium offers daily protection:

- Your pages are checked every day.

- Cost is $19.95/month for up to 10 pages.

- $1.00/month for each additional page.

More Online Content Providers to Consider

About
Associated Content
BrightHub
Content Divas
CrowdSpring
Daily Article
Demand Studios
Examiner
Gather
Human Rewriter
Livestrong

LoveToKnow
Mahalo
The Content Authority
Wikinut
WiseGeek
Worldvillage

Embrace Social Media

The rise and growth of social-networking sites, such as Facebook and Twitter, has been a societal tsunami. Facebook, founded by Mark Zuckerberg in 2004, now claims more than half a billion monthly users. And it has morphed into something more than simply a gabfest, a gossip forum. More and more businesses, including sole-proprietorships like you, are discovering that promotional and marketing opportunities abound in the social-networking arena.

Facebook & Twitter

Basic startup for Facebook and Twitter is the same: Create an account, link to your site, get optimum keywords in the title.

With Facebook, in addition to your standard profile page, you can create a Fanpage, which is more business or topic related. This is a growing trend: More and more businesses want a Facebook web address.

Once you get twenty-five people who like your Fanpage, you can shorten your URL to more closely identify with your business. For example, Blake's template site, Template Mill, has a Facebook address of www.facebook.com/templatemill. Before he acquired twenty-five "fans," his URL was far less memorable: www.facebook.com/profile.php?id=737723982.

In March 2011, Facebook instituted new procedures that make promotion even easier. Developers can now create what's called an I-Frame application, which lets you pull in web content, HTML content, from your site. Hosted on your server, it allows you to have a mini-website within your Facebook account. If you're selling something on your webpage, you can now have that text pop up on your Facebook page.

Increasingly, company ads are bypassing their websites and sending potential customers directly to Facebook. Ideally, though, you want to have both a website and a Facebook page. With the latter, you gain access to 500 million users, more and more of whom rarely venture outside of Facebook. Some even conduct their searches there. The company/person looking for writers or editors may check there before Google. If you build a Facebook presence—and put the right keywords in the title—they will come.

Though Facebook offers more flexibility, Twitter, too, can enhance your marketing potential. The biggest limitation: Twitter lets you post only 140 characters. But that may be enough if you simply want to announce a new product or service, or lure visitors to your site. Put up a tweet and link back to your page. As with Facebook, people can respond and interact.

Attracting Followers

Blake regularly relies on paid services to attract followers to his sites. Typically, he contracts with a company that then suggests to its thousands of followers that they go to his Facebook page. One such site, Fiverr (www.fiverr.com), features services that cost no more than five dollars. Blake has had success with Buy Bulk Likes (www. buybulklikes.com). Charges range from $5 to $50. As usual, you get what you pay for. Blake paid one service $5—and added exactly one follower. When he paid another service $50, he quickly gained 1,600 followers, all apparently interested in what his page had to offer.

You can find companies that will do the same for Twitter. (Check out Tweetbig.com.) Last year Blake created a Twitter account to pitch our book, *How to Self Publish the CreateSpace Way.* He chose an available title with optimum keywords: "Self Publish POD." (POD—Print on demand—is the publishing model CreateSpace follows.) After setting up an account with Tweetbig, he started the process of attracting visitors who were following similar Twitter accounts. One month later, he had attracted 5,000 followers. By the end of the second month, he had 9,000 followers.

Another valuable service is SponsoredTweets.com, a Twitter advertising platform that connects advertisers with tweeters. Sponsored Tweets requires that your Twitter account be active for sixty days and that you have at least 100 tweets. Once that happens, your Twitter account qualifies to offer sponsored tweets.

If your numbers rise high enough (Shaquille O'Neal has 4 million Twitter followers), advertisers will begin to approach you, asking to put their tweets on your site and paying for the privilege. You set the price per click—the more followers, the higher the price. Create several Twitter accounts, get even a couple of clicks per day, and you have created a revenue stream. It doesn't take much work, but you must post tweets at least every few days.

YouTube Videos

Gone are the days when YouTube videos featured little more than cute cats and Frisbee-catching dogs. Today, a growing number of companies are creating YouTube videos to market their products and services. That means they need creative people to write the storyboard, laying out each scene in detail.

Some videos are merely text, in the manner of a PowerPoint presentation. Still, companies need writers to create that sales copy. If you feel qualified, add those services to the ones you're already promoting on your website.

Another possibility is to make your own YouTube video and link back to your website. For example, when we produced a book and video to teach umpiring skills, we posted a clip on YouTube, entitled "You Be the Judge" (the title of our DVD). Then we added a link to our website (http://www.howtoumpirebaseball.com) in the description of the video.

Similarly, Blake recently built fifteen Amazon Affiliate sites, offering everything from golf gizmos to women's watches. For each, he put up a 25-30-second YouTube video, just music, text, images—and keywords.

Below each YouTube video, you can post a description and add a link to your site. If you employ keywords properly in your video title, Google searchers will find you; YouTube videos always come up in the first few pages of search results. And each video has its own page, so viewers can rate them, post comments, and interact with others doing the same. In this way, you create a buzz.

The potential upside of building a presence on social-networking sites was clearly evident with the most recent Charlie Sheen incident. While in the throes of yet another manic episode, he attracted more than a million Twitter followers in 24 hours, a new record. When he broke that record the next day, one company offered him $1.5 million a year to run their tweets through his site.

In Sum

Technology continues to make it easier to take advantage of social media. Blake now uses plugins that automatically take new content that he posts on his WordPress site and posts it on his Twitter page.

On Facebook, an application is now available that will pull new posts from your website and post them on your Facebook account. For example, on Blake's Greener Living Today site, he receives almost daily news reports on environmental issues. As those come in and post to greenerlivingtoday.com, they also post to his Twitter and Facebook sites—without his lifting a finger.

By now you should be able to see the benefits of marketing your writing skills and services using social-media sites.

Write an Ebook

An electronic book (also e-book, ebook, digital book) is a text and image-based publication in digital form produced on and read on computers and other digital devices. An ebook can begin as a conventional printed book, or be born digital. The *Oxford Dictionary of English* defines ebook as "an electronic version of a printed book," but more and more ebooks exist without any printed equivalent. Ebooks are usually read on dedicated hardware devices known generically as *e-Readers*. Personal computers and some cell phones can also be used to read ebooks.

U.S. libraries began providing free ebooks to the public in 1998 through their websites and associated services. At first, ebooks were primarily scholarly, technical or professional journals, and could not be downloaded. In 2003, libraries added free downloadable popular fiction and nonfiction ebooks to their catalogues. A 2010 study found that two-thirds of public libraries in the U.S. were offering ebooks.

In the second quarter of 2010, Amazon reported that sales of ebooks for its Kindle topped sales of hardcover books for the first time ever. In 2011, ebooks beat out both hardcover and paperback books. The gap continues to grow.

Advantages of Ebooks

- Generally cheaper than paper books.

- Instantly available. No need to drive to a bookstore or wait for shipping.

- Convenient. Load several volumes onto a portable reading device. Build a whole library of digital books.

- Ebook-reading software is free and easy to download from the Internet.

- Quick to download. The average novel takes only 3-4 minutes.

- More environmentally friendly—saves trees.

- Updating content is faster and cheaper—e.g., schools updating digital schoolbooks.

A Quality Ebook:

- Addresses the problems, concerns, needs, or desires of a well-defined target market.

- Stakes out a compelling position in the marketplace.

- Contains top-notch content.

- Offers great return on investment for buyers.

- Is supported by an effective marketing system.

- Is a meaningful extension of the relationship you've already created with your audience.

How to Write an Ebook

1. Choose a topic, preferably one you're passionate and knowledgeable about. What are your talents and skills? What can you teach others? Cake decorating? Rock climbing? How-to ebooks are among the best sellers.

2. Make an outline. Decide your major topics and then fill in the subtopics. Stay in chronological order if applicable.

3. Do your research. Find the facts to back up your ideas. Surf the Internet for articles and websites that support those ideas. Discover relevant resources to help your reader, such as forums, articles, and blogs. Save the links to these sites for later.

4. Write your ebook using MS Word or another word-processing software. If your ebook is very long, consider splitting it up into smaller ebooks on different subtopics. If the subject is cake decorating, the author might compose different ebooks on shaping cakes, ideas for children's birthday cakes, the art of icing, and cake recipes.

5. Ask others to proofread your ebook. Seek honest, constructive criticism. Make the necessary changes.

6. Consider adding interest with photos, your own if possible. If you lack photos, access photo sites, such as fotolia and iStockphotos.

7. Convert your document to a PDF file. You can find free online services, such as PDFonline. PDF Documents a) are more easily transmitted via email and downloads, b) look more professional, and c) are more difficult for others to copy.

8. Add links to your website, affiliate programs, blog, or online products. You can create an affiliate program and allow others to sell your ebook on their websites for a commission. You can give your ebook away as a free gift, knowing that readers will visit your links and may become your customer.

9. Make money from advertisers. If you have a website to promote your ebook, consider adding advertising to the site. A technique Blake uses is to obtain free software products and then offer to review those products in the ebook.

How to Sell an Ebook

Before you start selling your ebook, follow these steps:

1. **Nail down your offer**. What exactly are you selling? To avoid customer dissatisfaction, answer these questions before you start.

   ▪ Are you simply selling the downloadable ebook, or will you allow people some level of access before they buy? For example, you could offer a free download of part one, then charge for downloading part two.

• What rights do your customers get? Is the ebook for personal use only, or can they sell or transfer their copy of the ebook to others, as with Private Label Rights (PLR).

• How will you deliver the product? Over the Internet as a download? Or will you ship disks to your customers?

• What guarantees do you offer your customers?

• What level of support do you offer?

2. **Check your website.** Make sure your site clearly explains what you are offering.

3. **Decide on the price.** More art than science, pricing is nonetheless a critical part of your business plan. Underprice your ebook and you're throwing away money; overprice it and few will buy.

Some pricing ideas:

• Be guided by your competitors' prices.

• Start high and gradually cut the price until sales take off.

• Do market research. Ask people what they would pay.

Blake on pricing: "The prices of the ebooks I purchase are usually determined by the value of the information being offered. I've paid as much as $17 for an eight-page report, but it had the money-making information I needed."

SiteSell.com claims it can turn the "art" of pricing into a science: http://myps.sitesell.com.

4. **Get ready to accept payment.** You must accept payment by credit card or you could lose 90 percent of your potential orders. Find an automated system so you can concentrate on marketing rather than processing orders. To set up a fully automated system, you may need to make some minor adjustments to your site. Consider offering the following payment options, each with advantages and disadvantages.

▪ **PayPal.** PayPal is a service for sending and receiving money online. Blake used a merchant account for years before PayPal became what it is today. Now he uses PayPal almost exclusively. Its charges are comparable to merchant bank charges. PayPal has earned trust over the years and many people, including Blake, are more comfortable using PayPal than traditional merchant accounts. For example, if there's any question about the legitimacy of a credit-card charge, Paypal will put the order on hold until one of its human employees can look into it.

▪ **ClickBank.** ClickBank handles the processing of credit cards securely and sends you checks for your sales. ClickBank is especially good for selling ebooks, and it offers affiliate tracking at no extra cost. ClickBank is also good for digital-product sales because it provides the customer with an instant download of the product. Ebookcompiler.com offers a number of features that make it easy to sell your ebooks using ClickBank.

▪ **Merchant Account.** Merchant Accounts offer maximum credibility and flexibility, and the lowest fees per transaction. Acquiring your own Merchant Account may be the best option if you enjoy high sales volume, though many smaller sites, and even some larger ones, find ClickBank the better option. Establishing a Merchant Account may take a little more time and effort than the other options, and you may have to pay a monthly or annual fee just to maintain the account.

5. **Test Everything.** Before you unleash your sales website on the world, make sure everything works as it should. Test it once . . . then test it again. Ideally, run a test on a computer other than your own.

ClickBank

Here's the step-by-step process using ClickBank:

Step 1: Create a Digital Product

Let's say you love growing hollyhocks and have gained some expertise in the field. Now you want to share that expertise with others, maybe make some money in the bargain.

First, you need to create an ebook on the subject and develop a website to promote it. Then you need a way to attract customers and accept payments. That's where ClickBank comes in.

Step 2: Join ClickBank (clickbank.com)

ClickBank: a) has more than 100,000 active affiliate marketers ready to promote your ebook in exchange for a commission; b) offers order processing, fraud prevention, and customer support for digital products.

Step 3: Set Up a Product

You will work with ClickBank to set the retail price and the affiliate commission you wish to pay. Once that's set, you will submit your ebook to ClickBank for approval.

Step 4: Activate a Product

Once ClickBank approves your product, you pay a one-time $49.95 activation fee.

Your ebook is soon live in the ClickBank Marketplace and available for ClickBank affiliates to promote.

How to Sell Your Ebook on Kindle

Amazon Kindle is a technological device developed by Amazon.com for the rendering and displaying of ebooks and other digital media. Amazon's first hardware device, the Kindle First Generation, was released in the U.S. in November 2007.

In March 2009, Amazon.com launched an application called Kindle for iPhone, allowing iPhone and iPod Touch owners to read Kindle content on those devices.

With Kindle now available on so many different platforms, you should consider adding your book title to the Kindle catalog.

Setup. Setting up your title on Kindle is easy. Once you have an Amazon account, access Amazon's self-publishing area:

- Scroll to the bottom of any page on Amazon.com and click on "Self-publish with Us."

- In the navigation column on the left, click on "Kindle Books." This will take you to the Digital Text Platform section.

- Click on the "Sign in" button, located on the right side of the page.

- In the upper-left, click on "Add new item" to add your book title.

Here you are asked to provide the following information:

Product Details

- Title
- Description
- Author(s)
- Publisher
- ISBN
- Language
- Publication Date

Confirm Content Rights

- Define territories that you have rights in.
- Confirm that you own all rights.

Upload and Preview Book

Kindle will convert all elements in your doc file to the Kindle format. This will assign a default font style and convert any color to black and white.

The easiest way to get started on Kindle is to upload an MS Word doc file of your book. PDF files are now accepted, but the quality is unpredictable, and image quality is poor. If you desire a format viewable on multiple devices, consider using the eBook conversion services of companies such as Media Design Publishing (www.mediadesignpublishing.com), which will take your MS Word doc file and convert it accordingly.

Enter a Suggested Retail Price

Enter the price for the Kindle version of your book. Kindle pricing varies. Some Kindle versions are priced the same as the book itself; others are discounted as much as 50 percent or more. The price you set is a personal call, but because we didn't like creating competition for the sale of our printed books, we once suggested pricing the Kindle version close to the cover price. But that has changed, thanks to Amazon's new royalty structure. If your Kindle book is priced no higher than $9.99, you receive a royalty of 70 percent. Though most of our print books are priced around $14.95, we are now pricing our Kindle books at $9.99 and receiving roughly the same royalties we would if they were priced at $14.95. What's more, our Kindle sales are starting to surpass our print sales.

Enable Amazon Kindle Store

That's it! It usually takes a few days for the Kindle version of your book to appear in the Amazon catalog.

Copyright

If you live in the United State or European Union, your work is automatically covered by copyright, even if you do nothing. It can be helpful to affirm your copyright on your website and in your ebooks.

Consider obtaining a creative commons license. Creative commons licenses, which originated in 2002, include a range of copyright licenses that allow the distribution of copyrighted works, with varying limitations on that distribution.

What is an affiliate?

An affiliate is someone who promotes a product or service to potential customers, receiving a commission on each sale he or she generates.

Let's say with your growing interest in gardening, you buy an ebook you like through ClickBank about mulching, and you want to recommend it to others. You sign up for a free ClickBank account, then find the ebook about mulching in the ClickBank Marketplace. You create a customized HopLink and post it in places where you think people will be interested in the ebook—say, on your gardening blog, the gardening forum you're a member of, your Facebook profile, even in an email to your gardener friends.

If someone clicks on your HopLink and then buys the ebook, you get a commission on the sale. Depending on the product, commissions range from 1 percent to 75 percent (25 cents to $150).

Affiliates can promote as many products as they want. ClickBank handles all payment processing and commission tracking.

Sell Your Editorial Services

If you have the requisite writing/editing skills and can muster a resume that includes books or articles you've written or edited, along with some testimonials, consider starting a website to pedal your editorial services. One thing is certain: Plenty of writer wannabes in cyberspace could use the help.

Services you might offer include various levels of involvement in:

- Copyediting
- Manuscript evaluation
- Character analysis
- Plot analysis
- Query letters
- Book proposals
- Ghostwriting
- Book doctoring
- Proofreading
- Research
- Word processing
- Layout
- Consulting on self-publication

Copyediting

The heart of your client work will likely be copyediting. Because we all "learn" to write in the second grade, millions of people think they can do it just fine, without help. Every day a few find out otherwise, and they represent the potential audience for your services.

A good editor can take a clunky twenty-word sentence, cut eight words, and retain the meaning. Can you do that? Do you sense the power in the new, leaner version? If so, you may be qualified.

At all levels of copyediting—light, medium, and heavy-the copyeditor corrects errors, queries the author about confusing passages, requests advice when resolution is unclear, and prepares a style sheet.

Before you begin work, determine which level of editing the client wants.

Light Copyediting

- Correct faulty spelling, grammar, and punctuation.

- Correct incorrect usage (such as infer vs. imply).

- Check cross-references ("As Table 9 shows . . .").

- Ensure consistency in spelling, hyphenation, numerals, and capitalization.

- Check for proper sequencing (such as alphabetical order) in lists and other displayed material.

Medium Copyediting

- Perform all light copyediting tasks.

- Change text and headings to achieve parallel structure.

- Flag inappropriate figures of speech.

- Ensure that key terms are handled consistently.

- Ensure that previews, summaries, and end-of-chapter questions reflect actual content.

- Track the continuity of plot, setting, and character traits in fiction manuscripts.

- Change passive voice to active voice, as needed.

- Flag ambiguous or incorrect statements.

- Enforce consistent style and tone in a multi-author manuscript.

Heavy Copyediting

- Perform all medium copyediting tasks.

- Eliminate wordiness, triteness, and inappropriate jargon.

- Smooth transitions and move sentences to improve readability.

- Assign new levels to headings to achieve logical structure.

- Suggest—and sometimes implement—additions and deletions.

Note: In a heavy copyedit, the editor improves the flow of the words rather than simply ensuring correct usage and grammar. Instead of merely flagging problems, the editor may suggest recasts and may seek a uniform tone and focus, as specified by, say, the publisher.

Manuscript Evaluation

Sometimes a client will want you to read, not edit, a manuscript and evaluate it for readability or publishing potential. In a complete manuscript evaluation, you may weigh in on the following: clarity, plots and subplots, pace and story flow, dialogue, description, language, readability, organization, spelling, grammar, word usage, typos, punctuation, formatting, and character development.

Some questions to ask:

- Does the manuscript immediately grab a reader's attention (the hook)?

- Are the characters believable?

- Is the dialogue powerful? Authentic? Is there a good balance of dialogue and narrative?

- Has the writer chosen an effective point-of-view character or characters?

- Is the setting realistic?

- Does the plot hold together?

- How's the pacing?

Promoting Your Services

When Steve published his book, *How to Write Your Life Stories . . . Memoirs that People Want to Read,* he created a website, memoirwritings.com, to promote it. The website also offers a link to a page advertising his editing/ghostwriting services.

Besides creating your own promotional website, look for sites that offer a platform for posting freelance services, such as Elance (elance.com), Vworker (vworker.com), and Freelancer (freelancer.com).

Moreover, creating a presence on Facebook, Twitter, and other social-networking sites can help you attract an audience due to the targeted nature of their advertising platforms.

Consider joining Linkedin (linkedin.com), a professional network similar to Facebook's social network. Join one of the many writing groups that allow writers to share ideas and editors to attract new business.

Dealing with Clients

If a potential client finds you through your website, chances are he or she is a stranger. Before you commit to a project, you need to establish some trust. Try to meet with the client at least once, but if geography precludes that, talk on the telephone. Your business relationship will likely be email driven, but a verbal exchange can engender trust in a way that email cannot.

You don't have to like your client, but it helps. Be friendly, use appropriate humor to break the ice, and then get down to business. Ask specific questions: What are the client's goals? How can you help? Try to reach an agreement on duties, fees, and a payment plan. Consider signing a written contract, for, as someone said, "In a court of law, a verbal agreement isn't worth the paper it's printed on."

Before you commit to a project, make sure:

- The potential client knows what he or she wants to create. Steve was once hired by Maryann to ghostwrite a business book, working title: *How to be an Effective Executive Assistant*. At their first and only meeting, Steve asked Maryann to compose a table of contents or at least a list of chapter headings. "I don't think I can do that," she said. The fact that Maryann paid him a thousand dollars in advance blinded him to this red flag. After a few fitful months, the relationship fizzled out like a defective firecracker.

- You understand the depth of editing the client wants. Steve briefly worked with Sergio, an immigrant from Eastern Europe who wanted to write his memoirs. Though a learned man, Sergio struggled with English, and that was reflected in the first chapter he sent Steve for editing. Since he hadn't determined precisely what his client wanted, Steve tore into that chapter and edited it for maximum readability. The result was a sea of red ink. Sergio was offended and terminated the project. Though the client's response was mean-spirited, Steve blamed himself for not communicating better.

- You agree on financial matters. Early in his editing career, Steve was contacted by Hasan, a Moroccan American who wanted help writing his memoir about growing up in Morocco and immigrating to Florida. In his initial email, he asked whether Steve could edit a certain number of pages for $250. Steve responded that he didn't know, that it depended on the depth of editing needed, and that his rate was $50 per hour. Without ever finalizing an agreement, Hasan sent the manuscript and Steve began work. In the end, as you might now guess, Hasan refused to pay more than $250.

This points to an inescapable truth—some clients will try to cheat you. The author-editor relationship demands trust on multiple levels, including the financial one. Before you commit to anything, insist on speaking to the client face to face, or at least on the phone. Trust your instincts, but make no mistake: You can be fooled. Most of us are suckers for a charming huckster.

Payout

Rates vary widely, depending on various factors, including personal ones such as how desperately you want the work. Steve, who has edited and ghostwritten clients' work for years, charges $50 per hour, which is probably mid-range. If you have a sense of how long the project will take, consider offering a flat rate.

Find out what services the competition offers and what they charge. For example, check out: wordprocess.com, lorizueedits.com, the-draft-editor.com, firstediting.com, hyperlife.net.

Of course, it doesn't matter what you charge if no one finds your site.

Write a Blog

If you're a blogger wannabe, you face plenty of competition. By one estimate, 133 million blogs have surfaced on the Internet since 2002. Close to a million blogs are posted in any 24-hour period.

On the plus side, 346,000,000 people around the world read blogs in 81 languages, according to comScore, (March 2008).

Some people start a blog to entertain family and friends. Others want to inform or educate. Still others want to share opinions on music, books, films, politics, cooking, photography, and myriad other topics. Before you proceed, make sure you're clear about your motives. Why do you want to blog? Knowing the answer to that question will help you achieve your goals.

Here's how you can get started:

1. Choose a Good Blog Topic

Ask and answer these questions when deciding what to blog about:

- **How interested are you in the topic?** To go forward, the correct answer is "very."

- **Is the topic in demand?** It's much easier to ride a trend than to try to create demand out of thin air.

- **Does your topic have growth potential?** Will your topic grow in popularity or sizzle out quietly?

- **How many competitors will you face?** Google the topic and research the competition.

- **Do you have enough content?** Can you write compellingly on your topic at least three times a week?

- **Does the topic offer you a way to connect with your audience?** Your topic should help you forge connections with others and give you opportunities to be personal and share passions.

2. Read Other Bloggers' Work

With over a hundred million blogs in the blogosphere, chances are many of them are better than yours, especially if you're a beginner. Chances are they have higher page rank, more traffic, and come up earlier in search-engine results. Read a wide array of blogs and note what works and what doesn't. Why are some blogs more popular than others?

3. Make Comments on Other Blogs

Making relevant comments on other blogs should be part of the routine management of your own blog. It's a way of announcing your presence. Seize on any opportunities to promote your blogging efforts. For example, when posting on related forums, include links back to your blog in your signature, which is part of your profile. Continuous exposure increases the chances that other bloggers will create backlinks to your site. Backlinks are a big part of Search Engine Optimization.

4. Write Regularly

Write and post as regularly as possible—ideally at least three times a week for the search engine bots to crawl on your site. Search engines love to see content updates. And creating regular blog posts is the best way to improve your writing skills.

5. Learn Basic SEO

The most basic SEO involves using keywords. Use the Google Adwords Keyword Tool to determine the most searched keywords related to your blog content. Be clear about your purpose. Are the keywords for advertising, client backlinks, affiliate links, or what? Normally, weaving keywords organically into your text will suffice. Search-engine algorithms love natural phrasing and even mistakes, for that suggests a real human being compiled the content.

6. Mingle in Social Networks

Make use of social networks like Twitter, Facebook, and MySpace to market your blog. Applications and plugins exist that automatically post your recently written blog to your Facebook or Twitter accounts.

Consider other networks as well, such as DIGG, Delicious, Mister Wong, Spurl, StumbleUpon, and Technorati.

7. Press on

Building traffic for your blog, like building a business, requires mountain-climber perseverance.

8. Follow Your Passion, Not Profit

Blog on topics about which you have a burning passion. Give yourself at least a year to develop a following. When the traffic comes, the money will follow.

How Bloggers Make Money

So you want to make money in the blogosphere. You're not alone. More and more people are finding ways to squeeze profit from their blogs.

Many experts suggest blogging in relative anonymity for six months before turning pro. When you've improved your game and are ready to develop a money stream from your blog, consider the possibilities below. Keep in mind that not all blogs are created equal, and some streams may work better than others. Experiment with as many as possible and see what works best for you.

1. Google AdSense

For most bloggers, AdSense provides the most reliable and significant portion of their revenues. You can display image- and text-based ads.

2. Affiliate Programs

One of the biggest and best is Amazon's affiliate program. To join or get more information, click on the Join Associates link at the bottom of the Amazon home page.

Here are some tips for implementing a successful affiliate program:

▪ Know Your Audience

What might your readers be looking for as they surf by your blog. Specific products or services? What would trigger them to buy? Start with your readers in mind rather than the product.

▪ Make Honest Recommendations and Endorsements

Your readers return to your blog day after day because something about you or your site resonates with them. This suggests they have at least some level of trust and respect for you. A sure way to destroy that good will is to recommend they buy something you don't honestly believe in.

Says Darren Rowse, founder of ProBlogger (problogger.net): "The best results I've had from affiliate programs are where I give an open and honest appraisal of the product—including both its strengths and weaknesses."

Due to time constraints, you may choose to link to products and not review them. The same advice applies—be honest. Offering a link to a product is a tacit endorsement of that product.

▪ Link to Quality Products

Choose products and companies with good reputations and quality sales pages. After all, it's *your* reputation at stake, too.

▪ Add Contextual Links

If someone reading a post on a particular topic on your blog sees an ad for a related product, he is more likely to click it than if he saw an ad for something else. The same is true for affiliate programs. Consider multiple links throughout your blog that advertise products relevant for readers reading particular parts of your blog.

- **Position Links for Maximum Effectiveness**

Eye-tracking studies have identified areas of maximum interest on a webpage. These "hotspots" include the top of a sidebar, inside your content, and at the end of a post just above comments. The hottest of the hotspots is the upper-left corner, the so-called Golden Triangle.

- **Boost Traffic Levels**

Traffic levels are key to making money from almost any online activity. The more people who see your well-designed, well-placed, and relevant affiliate links, the more sales you will generate. So don't just work on your links—work on building a readership. Then figure out how to direct traffic on your blog toward the pages featuring your affiliate links.

- **Diversify without Clutter**

With countless products to link to, you will certainly want to offer more than one. But beware of cluttering your blog with too many links. You run the risk of a) diluting the effectiveness of those links and b) annoying your readership.

- **Don't Trick Your Readers**

Clearly label your affiliate links, so people know where they lead.

- **Follow Track Results**

Most affiliate programs offer some type of tracking system that allows you to see which links are effective. Note which link positions and labels work best, which products sell, and use the information to plan future affiliate strategies.

3. Book Sales

Write a book—ebook, hard copy, or both—on your blog topic and sell copies on your site. Make sure your URL is prominently displayed in your book.

4. Continuity Programs

A continuity program allows you to earn a recurring income from people who subscribe to a service you offer. Also called Membership Sites/Programs, they may include PLR articles, pre-built sites, and/or tutorial courses.

5. Direct Ads

These are advertisements, including banner ads and links, which you sell directly to sponsors.

6. Advertising Networks

If you apply to certain ad servers, they will give you code to put on your site that will display advertising based on the content of your site. Two such companies are Chitika and Kontera.

Chitika (chitika.com) is a full-service online advertising network serving over 3 billion monthly impressions on more than 100,000 websites. Chitika is an easy-to-use platform for earning daily ad revenue.

Kontera (kontera.com) is another popular contextual advertising program that links text to related advertising. They give you code for your page, and it actually spiders your content and links to keywords that are relevant to their advertisers.

7. Job Boards

Offering an online job board is low maintenance, provides a valuable service to visitors, and adds value to your blog. This application is available as a plugin or a data feed, and as an affiliate program.

8. Speaking Fees

If you develop expertise in a subject, someone may actually pay you to speak. Whether you are paid or not, speaking engagements offer opportunities to sell books and promote your blog.

10. Other Income

Check out smaller advertising programs, such as Infolinks, Direct Media Exchange, and Text Link Ads.

Blogging Platforms

Major blogging platforms include WordPress, TypePad, Blogger, LiveJournal, Tumblr, Multiply, and Xanga.

Blake favors WordPress for the control it offers. As a reminder, WordPress is an open-source blog-publishing platform powered by PHP and MySQL. Its many features include a user-friendly administration panel, a rich plugin architecture, and an advanced templating system.

The big advantage of WordPress is the control it gives the blogger. You own the domain; you set up the blog the way you want. TypePad, Blogger, and the others are popular social-media platforms owned by someone else, which means you have to follow their guidelines. On the plus side, they tend to enjoy high page rank and the search engines favor them. What's more, if you don't know how to set up your site, how to upload your files to the server, and don't want to mess with buying your domain, then choose a platform other than WordPress.

Beginners may benefit from taking a course on "Starting a Blog." At a minimum, such a course should cover how to:

- fine-tune your concept and make sure it works.

- find the right design and tone of voice.

- understand and use the available blogging platforms and tools.

- get your blog started and manage it at the right pace.

- add basic audio and visuals.

- use social tools to promote and grow your blog.

Write for Online Magazines

An online magazine (webzine, ezine, e-zine, electronic magazine, digital magazine) is more than just a blog. It is usually distinguished by its more stringent editorial approach. Online magazines typically have editors or editorial boards that review submissions and make sure all material meets the expectations of the publishers and the readership.

The largest print publishers usually provide digital versions of their print magazine titles, usually for a fee. Many general-interest online magazines provide free access to their content; others have opted to impose a subscription fee to access premium online articles and/or multimedia content. It's a reminder that ezine publishers that have embraced the interactive qualities of the Internet do more than simply duplicate the printed magazine on the web.

Some online magazines generate revenue from search ads targeted to visitors, banner (online display) ads, affiliations to retail websites, classified ads, product-purchase capabilities, and advertiser directory links.

Depending on the business model, the exposure a writer receives from writing for an online magazine can be great or small. One of the first and most successful, salon.com, founded in 1995, today reports 5.8 million unique visitors a month.

How to Query an Online Magazine

- Pursue topics that spark your passion.

- Search for publications likely to appreciate your expertise. Start with online magazines that you currently read. Publications like *Writer's Market* (writersmarket.com) can help you locate other potential online publications. Create a list of those that might be a candidate for your work.

- Study the writer's guidelines for the publications you choose. Visit each potential market's website and click the link that says "submissions," "employment," or the like. Read and follow the guidelines. Note: a) when submissions are accepted, b) from whom, c) about what, d) in what format, and e) with what additional requirements. Some require online submission forms; others prefer you send materials via snail mail. Some welcome simultaneous submissions (submitting the same article to more than one publisher); others forbid that practice.

- Send either a query letter or the complete article, as per the guidelines. Most publications prefer a query, a letter stating what you plan to write, how you plan to write it, and why you're supremely qualified to do it.

- Be persistent and patient. Keep researching and sending queries at least every week. Direct your query letter to the current editor of the publication.

- Be patient with editors you've already contacted; they are often swamped. Give them a couple of weeks before sending a polite follow-up.

- Some publications will request the complete article, usually via email. Be cautious about sending out your work before you have a contract.

The Query Letter

A query letter, or query, is an offer to write an article and an attempt to interest an editor in publishing it. It is, in other words, a sales pitch.

Instead of writing an entire article that might not be bought, you write a letter about the proposed article. Your goal: a commitment to buy, or at least a strong expression of interest. By drumming up sufficient interest in advance, you save yourself the grief of researching and writing things no one wants to publish. Also, by determining which publication is going to publish the finished article, you can more clearly envision and target your readers when you finally write it.

Include the following in your query letter:

- Your idea. What the idea is about. For example: "The Tasadays are the most primitive tribe living in the world today."

- Your slant. "The Tasadays have a more satisfying life than more civilized groups of people."

▪ Your treatment. Some indication of how you intend to approach the subject. "I will build the article around interviews with several notable Tasadays."

▪ Sources. Some of the ways you will acquire information. "Several Tasadays have moved into my neighborhood, and I've become friendly with them. Moreover, I have been granted access to the Tasaday cave drawings in the Philippines . . ."

▪ Make the editor care. "I believe the readers of *Caveman Digest* will be interested in this piece because of their close philosophical ties with the Tasadays. In a recent study of value systems among Cavemen and Tasadays, professor Seth Loo found remarkable similarities between . . ."

▪ Your writing credits. "My work has appeared in *Firehouse* magazine and *Humpty Dumpty* . . ." Don't write something like "I've never published anything, but . . ." or "I'm taking a writing class and this is my first query." Such remarks will only encourage an editor to reject you.

▪ Suggested length and deadline. "I propose an article of approximately 2,000 words, and I can deliver it within two months." If the editor likes your idea, she will suggest a length and deadline of her own.

▪ Other relevant information about yourself. "I am half Tasaday myself, and for three years I was editor-in-chief of a Manila newspaper, where I came in contact with many Tasadays." Avoid the irrelevant: "I am married, have three children, and a frog named Butch."

Other Tips

▪ The letter should be brief—no more than two pages; one is better.

▪ Single-space the letter; double-space between paragraphs.

▪ Your letter should contain the above information but in no special order. Also, you are not necessarily dead if you leave out one item.

▪ Make the query interesting. It should entertain, inform, and compel. Most important, it should make the editor want to read on. Make it lively to demonstrate your enthusiasm, factual to demonstrate your knowledge, and well written to demonstrate your talent.

▪ Use anecdotes, quotes, examples, statistics, questions, jokes, excerpts from other articles, and whatever else it takes to show the editor what you want to write, how you want to write it, why you are the person to write it, and why the editor should care.

- Make the lead grabby, but don't overpromise. Don't write, "The Midwest's greatest tragedy occurred in Corn Hollow, Iowa—and yet few people outside of Corn Hollow know about it," if the tragedy was, say, a man falling into a vat of chocolate.

- Spell the editor's name correctly; in fact spell everything correctly.

- If you have previously published works, include or refer to them. These are called tear sheets. Ideally, they are similar to the writing you are proposing.

- If photos are available, say so.

- Finish politely and affirmatively. "Thank you for your attention. I look forward to hearing from you."

- Make the whole package neat and professional.

Results

- Nothing happens. Wait a couple of weeks, then write to the editor, politely reminding her who you are and asking for an update.

- Rejection. You may see two types of rejections: form and letter. In a letter rejection, try to find encouragement in the editor's words; listen carefully to any constructive criticism.

- A go-ahead on speculation. This is encouraging—the editor is showing interest—but you have a decision to make. You may write the piece and find the editor still doesn't want it.

- Firm assignment. Write back your acceptance. Open celebratory beverages.

How to Write for an Online Magazine

Some writers shun online magazine because they see them as somehow less significant than print magazines. But with the contraction of the print-magazine market, online magazines are increasingly essential to any writer's portfolio.

Consider these issues when writing for an online audience.

1. Be Keyword Savvy

Online magazines will often ask you to include keywords in text and title for search-engine optimization. Though the process may seem forced at first, you'll soon learn where to insert them into your copy.

Say you're writing an article about photography. You may have to include the words *photography* and *photographer* more frequently than you might otherwise, but a good writer can weave them seamlessly into the text.

Prominent online magazines often have special editors who'll add keywords for you once the final draft is received. That takes the pressure off the writer.

2. Be Sensitive to Online Readers

When you write for a print magazine, you are targeting a specific audience created and developed by the magazine itself. Write for an online magazine, however, and your potential audience is not only that magazine's specified readership but also search engines and social media. You have to learn how to craft your articles so that they appeal to all three.

Online readers, typically younger and more media-savvy than those reading print journals, expect your articles to be accompanied by visually arresting photos, videos, and/or sound files. As a freelancer, it may be up to you to find those.

Says Nick Clarke, founder of *Gunpowder Magazine* (gunpowder-magazine.com): "Even when I find an amazing story that's suitable for *Gunpowder*, if I can't find gorgeous photography to back it up I won't publish it . . . it's as simple as that."

3. Check Your Facts

Although you are writing for a medium that can be edited after print with the click of a button, that doesn't excuse sloppy journalism. Your readers have the greatest research tool in history at their fingertips, and you can bet some will check your facts. Don't let them prove you wrong.

4. Stay Ahead of the Curve

When approaching online magazines for work, freelancers need to stay ahead of the curve. That means spending hours researching the latest trends, which are ever changing.

Some publishers are interested only in late-breaking ideas and set deadlines measured in hours. Not all online magazines are that time-sensitive, but those that rely on the hottest news want their freelancers to be one step ahead of the editors.

5. Consider Working Gratis

Some online magazine—and most online creative-writing magazines—pay their writers nothing. Which means you have a decision to make. Writing for free markets gives you experience and boosts your credibility in the online publishing world. For most writers, working for free is part of the "dues-paying" process.

How to Start and Run an Online Magazine

Launching a print magazine can take millions of dollars in capital; starting an online magazine may cost only a few hundred bucks. That helps explain why new online magazines are appearing every day on every subject imaginable, from dog grooming to ice climbing. Some are started by print publishers moving online, others by small businesses. But most are started by individuals with specialized knowledge or at least a deep passion for their subject.

An online magazine should have a well-defined focus and a variety of content. Like their print cousins, they are usually a mix of news, opinion, feature articles, reviews, interviews, and profiles.

Running an online magazine is one of the easiest enterprises available to individuals and small businesses. But if you want to create an online magazine with a professional design, with the functionality necessary to generate multiple revenue streams and the flexibility to grow, then you will require more professional solutions.

Free solutions offering limited functionality include Blogger.com and WordPress.com. Midrange solutions that offer professional design, payment processing, and flexible functionality start at around $2,000. One such: SubHub (www.subhub.com).

A less-expensive option is to set up a WordPress site and pay for the hosting of your own domain. Even if you pay someone to set it up, it should cost no more than $500, plus monthly hosting charges, which can be as low as $7 per month for one domain. HostGator offers hosting for unlimited domains for $8 per month. Pay for a year in advance, and you may cut the price in half.

The Steps to Success

Preliminaries

- Choose a subject.

- Research the competition.

- Select a business name.

- Buy a suitable domain name.

- Decide how your online magazine will generate income.

- Write a business plan.

- Design a content plan.

- Write the introductory pages.

- Create the first content, including articles, video clips, podcasts, etc.

Design

- Sketch out the layout.

- Plan the navigation.

- Create a design. Or choose a template design that fits your needs.

Creation

- Choose a platform.

- Specify the website functionality.

- Add the design to the platform.

- Add background content.

- Add the first articles.

- Implement payment processing.

- Integrate additional functionality.

Launch

- Test all links.

- Test payment processing.

- Test subscription and renewal process.

- Go live!

On Creating Content

A traditional magazine is published on a regular basis—monthly, bimonthly, quarterly, or less often. An online magazine, on the other hand, can add new articles and features whenever they become available, though some still adhere to deadlines and schedules. Online articles, whether written by the publisher, staff writers, or freelance writers, should relate to the general theme of the magazine. For example, if your online magazine is about health and wellness, you might include articles about exercise, fitness, diet, mental health, and other relevant subtopics. If your expertise is horses, write about horses, yes, but also ranch life, farm life, sports, racing, gambling, and pets. Use search engines and consult publications such as *Writer's Digest* and *Poets & Writers* for market ideas.

How to Make Money with an Online Magazine

Although print magazines charge consumers for subscriptions, most of their income comes from advertising, and so it is with online magazines. Contact companies that pedal products of interest to your readers and sell them advertising space. With an online magazine, that usually means banner ads or other space near the website content.

Developing Traffic to the Website

Traffic, of course, is what advertisers look for. You boost traffic with SEO practices, including:

- Backlinking
- Hard text links
- Referrals
- Advertising your new site
- Subscriptions

Ad Types

Traditional advertising. The advertiser pays a set fee to have a specified ad appear in the magazine for a set period of time.

Affiliate advertising. The advertiser doesn't pay an upfront fee but rather a percentage of a sale or a set price each time a customer makes a purchase through a particular advertisement.

Pay-per-click advertising. The advertiser pays the publisher a set amount each time a visitor clicks on an ad, regardless of whether a purchase is made.

Another method is charging by the ad banner impressions, usually a set cost per thousand (CPM) impressions.

Write Online Press Releases

The centerpiece of any public-relations effort has long been the press release. Press releases remain the number-one tool for communicating company news to the media. The press release itself has remained remarkably unchanged over the years—until recently. Today, all press-release-type materials must go digital. And they must be written in SEO style to be effective.

Press releases must have a clear, timely, newsworthy angle, and be free of advertising hype, direct address, and spam. Press releases should incorporate the following features/qualities:

Newsworthy Content: Include timely information about a new product or service, a business development or recent event, a milestone like an anniversary or award, or an expert opinion on a newsworthy subject. Don't use your press release for advertising.

Objective Tone: Press releases should be free of hype. Avoid any direct address (you, I, we,) unless used within a quotation from an organization's spokesperson. Direct address is a flag that the content is an advertisement rather than a news release. And creating emphasis with so called hype flags—exclamation points, all CAPS, effusive product/service claims—weakens your credibility.

Appropriate Length: Most press releases are between 300 and 600 words. Press releases that are overly short or long may not be indexed in the search engines.

Standard Grammar and Spelling: Press releases should be free of spelling and grammatical errors. Although jargon and acronyms are often good for search-engine ranking, you should include necessary definitions so the layman can understand.

Proper Formatting: Press releases may not contain HTML tags or formatting such as non-standard characters, tables, or forced line breaks.

Legal Accuracy: For press releases referencing legal action or criminal matters, you should include a case number, court of record, complaint number, or other sufficient documentation.

Avoid the following in your press releases:

Advertisements: A good press release informs the media and the general public about a newsworthy topic. If your press release reads like an advertisement, rewrite it.

Intent to Harm: Avoid content intended to harm or exact personal revenge against a person or group. Opinions should be appropriately attributed and should not contain unsubstantiated allegations or excessive hyperbole.

Sexually Explicit Content: Press releases should not contain references or links to explicitly sexual material, illegal material, or profane language.

SPAM: Too many of the wrong words will run you afoul of content filters. The wrong words include words and phrases frequently found in advertisements, in SPAM, and on non-newsworthy websites. Examples include *girls, amazing, FREE, sex, naked, make money,* and *don't miss this opportunity,* as well as anything to do with health supplements or pharmaceuticals for sexual enhancement.

Link SPAM: Limit your link count to 1 per 100 words.

Blog Posts: Blog posts, general-interest articles, "open letters," and the like usually lack attribution and news value, and are not an acceptable press-release format.

Opinion Pieces: News releases can be *about* a person or group's opinion on a topical subject, but should not contain only opinion. Opinions not attributed to a source are flags that the content may be an advertisement or opinion column rather than a news release.

Reprints: Your press release should not include feature articles, opinion columns, editorials, or news stories from other websites or publications, especially if they are copyrighted.

Fiction: Submit only accurate information.

Duplicate Content: Neither search engines nor readers want to see the same release more than once.

Online Gambling: Many sites will not publish releases that promote or link to online gambling, fantasy sports, and the like.

How to Write a Press Release

1. Write the headline. It should be brief, clear, and to the point, a compact version of the press release's key point. It may describe the latest achievement of an organization, a recent newsworthy event, or a new product or service. For example, "Disney opens theme park in Bangladesh." Note: Some prefer to write the headline after the text.

- Make the headline bold and larger than the press-release text.

- Write the headline in present tense. It's also common to exclude "a" and "the" and forms of the verb "to be." Thus, "Disney will open a theme park" becomes "Disney opens theme park."

- Cap the first word in the headline and all proper nouns. Do not capitalize every word.

- One way to create a headline is to craft an attention-grabbing statement from the most important keywords in your press release. That will a) boost your ranking with search engines, and b) make it easier for journalists and readers to quickly grasp what will follow.

Write the main copy. The press release should be written as you want it to appear in a news story.

- Start with the date and city in which the press release originated.

• The first sentence should grab the reader and say concisely what is happening. The next 1-2 sentences then expand upon that lead.

• Avoid fancy language, jargon, repetition, and overly long sentences and paragraphs.

• The first paragraph—usually two or three sentences—should sum up the press release, and further content should expand on it.

• Emphasize facts, such as events, products, services, people, targets, goals, plans, and projects.

Other Tips

Communicate the 5 Ws and H: *Who, what, when, where, why,* and *how.* First, answer these questions:

• What is the actual news and who is involved? Detail the people, products, items, dates, and other relevant newsworthy facts.

• Where does it take place?

• How will it happen?

• Why is it news?

From your answers, construct paragraphs and assemble them sequentially. The more newsworthy you make the press release, the greater your chances of having it picked up by journalists.

Watch your timing. The timing of a press release is critical. It must be recent news. If the press release is for immediate release, you may write IMMEDIATE RELEASE in all caps in the left margin, directly above the headline. A release with no release date is presumed to be for immediate release.

Include information about the company. Include the company name in the headline, in any subhead, and in the first paragraph.

Provide links. Provide information links that support your press release. In most cases, you will highlight the keyword(s) you'd like linked within the body content and then click on the link icon. You will then provide the link's URL and a title, such as "My Website." The words you choose for your links (anchor text) are important for SEO purposes.

Consider including images and/or video in your news release.

Signal the end of the press release with three # symbols, centered directly beneath the last line of the text.

Read other press releases on the web and note the tone, language, structure, and format of an effective press release.

Include a "call to action." What do you want the public to do with the information you are releasing? Buy a product? Then include information on where the product is available. Visit your website? Include the URL and contact information.

Paste the release into the body of the email, rather than attaching it. If you must use an attachment, make it a plain text or Rich Text Format file. Word documents are acceptable at most outlets, but if you are using the newest version (.docx), save down a version (.doc). Newspapers are on tight budgets and many have not upgraded. Use PDF files only if you are sending a full media kit with lots of graphics.

Make your headline the subject line of the email. Ideally, this will help your message stand out.

Companies that offer press-release writing services include Constant Content (constant-content.com) and eReleases (ereleases.com).

Become a Google News Publisher

In 2010, Blake set out to become a Google News publisher. His aim: to offer a press-release service on his Google News site. For a fee, he would post a press release for a company with the promise that it would show up in Google's top ten for its primary keywords.

Google News requirements back then were looser than now. The company looked the other way when you pre-populated your new site with press releases, a common way of priming the pump and getting content up quickly. Like others before him, Blake predated press releases within WordPress, making it look as if they'd been posted every day or so for the previous eight weeks. After that he and his wife began writing original news content to the tune of three articles per day. Blake created a regular monthly schedule that detailed what types of articles would appear on different days of the week. Monday might feature health, finance, and entertainment; Tuesday, sports, travel, and environment.

Once he had posted original content for a two-week period, Blake applied and went through the multilayered review process. He made it to the last step and was waiting to be indexed in the Google News database. After three weeks with no word, he contacted Google. That caused them to scrutinize his site, after which they canceled him because his site was preopoulated with press releases. "I was victimized by Google News's sudden change in policy," says Blake.

Blake, who is involved in dozens of online projects, chose not to reapply to Google News, but he remains optimistic about its money-making potential. "If you stay with it and pass through every review gate, you have a chance to make real money," he says. "But you have to treat it as a business. You have to put up original content—real news—every day or so, at least 250 words per article, keyword targeted. If you can do that, chances are your traffic will soar. Thousands and thousands of unique visitors will visit your news site every day, and some will click on your ads."

Here's how to get started:

Step One: Create Your News Site

First you need a domain name and a place to host your site. One option is HostGator, where you can register your domain name and set up an account all at once for $8.95 a month. HostGator accounts have what is called cPanel, and cPanel includes a feature that allows you to install a new WordPress site in less than a minute. This is the easiest way to create your new site.

If you have experience setting up a WordPress site, then go for it. If not, WordPress has an online installation guide: http://codex.wordpress.org/Installing_WordPress.

Once you have WordPress installed, you need to install your news theme. WordPress is compatible with a variety of themes that will enhance the look and design of your site. Although thousands of themes are free, Blake tends to gravitate toward higher-quality themes, usually costing $25 to $75. It's your choice. Higher-quality themes are usually better optimized for search engines by making good use of title and header tags (<h1> to <h6> tags are used to define HTML headings), but all WordPress coding is clean and favored by search engines.

For Google News sites, we recommend that you use a theme design that displays content in a news format. Blake still builds news sites, though not for Google News, and he uses the Advanced Newspaper theme by Gabfire Themes. The cost is $59, but it presents the content in a professional manner. Go to: http://www.gabfirethemes.com/advanced-wordpress-newspaper-theme.

To learn more about themes and free downloads, visit the WordPress site at www.wordpress.org.

Step Two: Set up Categories

Include a variety of categories on your site. This gives you the freedom to write about the newest hot topic, whatever it is. And sites that cover a wider range of news categories are more likely to be accepted by Google News. After your first site is accepted, you can create other sites that target a specific niche—say, a financial-news site or a sports-news site.

In your WordPress admin section, add at least these basic categories:

- Business
- Entertainment
- Featured News
- Finance
- Health
- Shopping
- Sports & Recreation
- Travel

Step Three: Make Google-News-Compatible Permalinks

Permalinks define the URLs added to your news stories or articles. Google News requires that each of these URLs contain a random number with at least three digits.

> The URL for each article must contain a random number consisting of at least three digits. For example, Google News can't crawl an article with this URL:
>
> http://www.medianewsandreports.com/news/article99.html.
>
> But it can crawl an article with this URL:
>
> http://www.medianewsandreports.com/paramount-sony-score-big-in-oscar-nominations-reuters/584105/

Note: If the only number in the article is an isolated four-digit number that resembles a year, Google News won't be able to crawl it. For example:

http://www.medianewsandreports.com/news/article2006.html.

Here's how to add permalinks:

- Log into your WordPress admin section and click on "Settings" on the left side. Below the Settings heading, you will see several subcategories. Click on "Permalinks."

- At the top of the Permalinks Settings page, click on "Common Settings."

- There you will see several choices, each with a check-mark box. Click on "Custom Structure."

- In the Custom Structure field, paste the following text: /%postname%/85%post_id%/

- Click the "Save Changes" button.

Congratulations—you just accomplished two things: 1) You changed the URLs of your posts to include the post title, which will help in general search-engine optimization; 2) you added a post number to the URL, thereby conforming to Google News requirements.

Step Four: Download Essential Plugins

One of the many benefits of using WordPress is that it allows for plugins, and there are thousands of them. Some cost money, but most are free.

Installing a plugin to your WordPress site is easy:

- Once you download the "Must Have" plugins, log into your WordPress admin section and click on the "Plugins" link on the left side of the menu bar.

- Once that page loads, click on the "Add New" button at the top.

- A text menu appears at the top of the page. Click on the link that says "Upload."

- Navigate to the plugin you want to load; activate it by clicking the "Activate Plugin" link that appears. Some plugins require an initial setup.

Below are some useful free plugins that you can download to your computer's hard drive. Note: Do not unzip the files; upload them to WordPress in their zipped format.

Google News Sitemap Generator. The sitemap this plugin will generate is specific to Google News. Google News has some specific rules and this sitemap generator will take care of them.

Meta Tag Generator. Your new site will have to be added to Google Webmaster Tools. To do that, you have to add a special Meta Tag to your site that Google will provide. This plugin was created because WordPress does not allow you to add Meta Tags.

Secure Form Mailer Plugin for WordPress. Google News requires a contact page, and this is the most popular plugin for creating contact forms in WordPress.

SEO Smart Links. This plugin is used to create more revenue streams for your blog.

WP Super Cache. This plugin creates a cache of every page that gets accessed by a visitor. Caching is basically taking a photograph of a page when the first person visits that page. That photograph is then presented to the visitors that follow. This serves two purposes: 1) It makes pages on your site load faster, and 2) it saves you from getting suspended by your hosting service. Occasionally, you may post an article that gets extremely high traffic in a short period; without this plugin, the server load would be huge and your host might suspend your account.

Step Five: Set up Your Organizational Structure

To gain approval as a Google News Source, you must look like an organization rather than a lonely soul banging out news articles from a tiny apartment, which you may in fact be. Here's how to look bigger than you are:

▪ Google News requires that your site have multiple authors, so create some pen names for yourself. Add those names as users in your WordPress admin area. Use those names when you post articles.

▪ Add an Authors page. Click on the "Pages" link in your admin section; then click on "Add New."

▪ The title of this page should be "Writers." This is where you list a) your pen names and b) a unique email address for each of them (or a link to a contact form).

▪ You have the option of adding a short bio under each name. If you actually have writers, you should do this.

▪ Create an About Us page. Click on the "Pages" link; then click on "Add New" in your admin section.

▪ Create a Privacy Policy page.

Here's an example of a Privacy Policy page:

Your Privacy
Your privacy is important to us. To better protect your privacy we provide this notice explaining our online information practices and the choices you can make about the way your information is collected and used. To make this notice easy to find, we make it available on our homepage and at every point where personally identifiable information may be requested.

Collection of Personal Information
When visiting _____, the IP address used to access the site will be logged along with the dates and times of access. This information is purely used to analyze trends, administer the site, track users' movement, and gather broad demographic information for internal use. Most important, any recorded IP addresses are not linked to personally identifiable information.

Links to Third-Party Websites
We have included links on this site for your use and reference. We are not responsible for the privacy policies on these websites. You should be aware that the privacy policies of these sites may differ from our own.

Changes to this Privacy Statement
The contents of this statement may be altered at any time, at our discretion.

• Create a Contact Us page. This may be another list of your authors with their email addresses and a company email address. You may also include a form that allows visitors to message you. If so, you will use the plugin, called Secure Form Mailer Plugin for WordPress, which you installed earlier.

Step Six: Post Your First Articles

Before applying to become a Google News Source, you must have a history of providing news online. That means you need to get content up on your site quickly. As stated above, you can no longer prepopulate your site with press releases, so what to do? A lot of publishers outsource the writing and backdate it in the same manner once used with press releases. Be careful that the assigned dates correspond to the actual news events.

Once you have enough articles for every category, add them to your site:

• Click the "Posts" link in your WordPress admin section.

• Click the "Add New" link.

• Add the title and contents of your first article.

▪ Add a picture. Google requires that you include an image in each news post. You can usually find relevant images at Google Images. (Google News prefers the jpeg format.) Another source is FreeDigitalPhotos.net. But the company requires that you list it as the image source. We recommend using a source such as FreeDigitalPhotos in order to avoid copyright issues. To upload an image, place your cursor before the first letter in the body of your article and click on the pic icon above the title field. When you get to the alignment option, choose "Left." That will place your picture in the top left of your article, with the text wrapped around the photo.

▪ Before you click the "Publish" button, select the category in which your article belongs. Check the appropriate category, but also check the Featured News category. Featured News is not mandatory later on, but for now let's add all posts to this category as well. The Featured Articles stand out on the site when Google is reviewing your content.

▪ In the field marked "Post Tags," add relevant keywords or keyphrases, separating each with a comma.

▪ Click the "Add" button next to the Post Tags field.

▪ Next, backdate your articles. Just above the Publish button on the right side, look for "Publish Immediately." Next to it, click on "Edit." A calendar will appear. For your first set of articles (one for each category), set the date to ten weeks ago. Then click the "Ok" button.

- Click the Publish button.

- After you post your first article, click "Posts" on the left navigation bar. You should see two articles: the one you just posted and another sample article titled "Hello World." Delete the Hello World post.

- After you finish backdating the first set of articles, start backdating the second set, this time changing the date to nine weeks ago. Repeat this pattern until you get to the current week.

- If you have no experience as a writer, you can find recent news stories in each of your categories (from Google News, MSNBC, CNN, etc.) and rewrite them. Your articles should be at least 150 words. Add a new article in each of your categories at least every other day, alternating so new content is always appearing on the site. You can do this by backdating or postdating in one sitting, or by posting them in real time.

Step Seven: Place Your First Ads

Any WordPress theme you choose will offer opportunities to place banner ads. Don't fill those spots with AdSense ads. Google News has no problem with your using Google AdSense ads, but before you are approved you want to appear as though you have paid advertising already in place and that yours is not a "made for AdSense" site.

Step Eight: Do a Final Site Check

When you think you're ready to become a Google News Source, take a final look at your site. Go through all the pages and ask yourself, "Does this look professional?" If not, make the necessary changes. Seek the opinions and advice of others.

Maybe the most common mistake potential Google News publishers make is to post articles written in a less than professional, or even semi-professional, manner. Reviewers at Google News pore over each article, and if they don't meet quality guidelines your site won't be accepted.

Step Nine: Apply to Google News

Once you're confident your site looks right, it's time to apply for inclusion in Google News.

Early in the process, you will face a question that asks if you're a representative of the site. Click the "Yes" button. That will open up the questionnaire form:

How many authors and editors contribute to the creation of your news content? Select either 6-10 or 11-20.

Contact information available on your site: Input the URL of the Contact Us page that you created earlier. Go to your site's homepage, click on the Contact Us page, and copy and paste the URL.

List of authors and editors available on your site: Paste the URL of the Writers page you created earlier.

Site location information: Be accurate here.

Content Type: Check the box that says "A Site."

Your contact information: Do not use a fake name here.

Subject: Type in "Google News Source Application."

Other comments: Write a letter that begins "Dear Google" or "To Whom It May Concern." Explain that you are applying to be a Google News Source. Detail any experience that you or your writers have. Be creative—they won't do a background check. Tell them that you believe your site has met all of the technical requirements and that you will be submitting a Google News Sitemap. Invite them to notify you of any technical problems or if they have any questions about you or the site.

Step Ten: Keep Posting Articles

During the application process, it's imperative that you add at least three fresh news articles to your site every day. These articles must be original and timely. At least one should deal with a current event.

Step Eleven: Submit a Google News Sitemap

A sitemap is a detailed text map of the hierarchy of all the categories, pages, and content on your website. Everything is linked with the URL of each, which enhances the search engines' ability to crawl a site.

The sitemap includes the URLs of the category pages, individual articles, archives, etc.

Here's a typical entry in a Google News Sitemap:

```
<url>
<loc>http://www.medianewsandreports.com/upping-th
e-ante-for-cliff-lee-wall-street-journal/583758/</loc>
  <n:news>
    <n:publication>
      <n:name>Media News and Reports</n:name>
      <n:language>en</n:language>
    </n:publication>

<n:publication_date>2010-12-09</n:publication_date>
    <n:title>Upping the Ante for Cliff Lee - Wall
Street Journal</n:title>
    <n:keywords>Sports</n:keywords>
  </n:news>
</url>
```

Note how it is separated into location (URL), news publication name, language, date, title, and tags (keywords).

Here's how to set up and submit a Google News Sitemap:

- You should have already installed the Google News Sitemap Generator (Step Four). To set up the sitemap, go to your WordPress admin section and click on the "Settings" tab at the bottom of the left-side navigation. A tree should open below it.

- Click on "Google News Sitemap." This will open the Settings page for the sitemap generator.

- Once the Sitemap Options page loads, make sure only two boxes are checked: 1) "Include posts in Google News sitemap" and 2) "Use post tags as sitemap keywords."

- None of the categories should be checked for exclusion at this time. If you have posted an editorial category or something that isn't newsy, you may want to exclude it. Google News doesn't like editorials unless you're well known.

- Now click the "Update Options" button. Here you can update the sitemap when new posts are added.

- The URL of your sitemap should be YourSite.com/google-news-sitemap.xml. Check that your sitemap is there. The plugin should work without problems; if not, contact the developer of the plugin.

▪ If your Google News Sitemap appears, it's time to submit it to Google. Most people already have a Google account. If not, simply sign up for Gmail and you will get one. Then sign in to your Google account and click on Settings > Google Site Settings.

▪ Find "Webmaster Tools" in the main menu. Add the site to the webmaster tools so that Google can keep track of everything. You will need to verify it by placing a special meta tag on your website that Google will provide. Use the Meta Tag Generator plugin to add the meta tag to your WordPress site.

▪ Once your site is verified, click on Site Configuration >> Site Maps. Click on the button that says "Submit a Sitemap," and enter "google-news-sitemap.xml."

▪ Once you submit the news sitemap, you will see an hourglass next to it. That hourglass will eventually turn to a red X. That's because news sitemaps are accepted only for sites actually in the Google News database. Once you are approved, the X will become a check-mark.

Step Twelve: Once Approved

You should hear back from Google News within a week, but it may take a month or more. Be patient. If your site is not approved, Google News will help you to overcome the problems. You might also tap into some online forums for tips. After you address the problems Google News listed, reply to their email, detailing the changes you made.

Once approved, you will receive an email that says your site will be spidered within four weeks or so. But it often happens much quicker than that, sometimes within a week. While you're waiting, keep posting at least three articles a day.

Some Ways to Profit as a Google News Source

1. Emphasize High-Paying Niche News Articles. Most of the 20,000 or so Google News Sources concentrate on breaking news stories. Very few are focused on one specific niche. If you write about celebrities, you may find you get a lot of traffic but not many clicks and not much money per click. If you write about politics or war or the latest earthquake, you will be swallowed up by the big news agencies. Instead, find and write about topics that generate high traffic, less competition, and high click-throughs.

Here are some possibilities:

Legal
Banking and Finance
Medical
Jobs
Technology
Education
Automobile
Fitness
Travel
Social Networking
Fashion

2. Make Your Ads More Alluring. For example, AdSense allows you to change the colors of your ads. Find the winning combination of ad placements and color variations.

3. Get Others to Write for You for Free. Solicit bloggers as guest writers on your Google News Source site. You can offer them a link to their blog in exchange for a quality newsworthy article about their niche, which may be a high-paying one.

4. Make Good Use of AdSense. AdSense is the main moneymaker for these types of sites.

5. Charge for Your Services Whenever Possible. Writers and SEO companies will approach you to post their content, allowing you to charge a fee for those services.

Wrap-up

Since we began writing this book, the Internet has, predictably, continued to grow. The economy has . . . well, it depends upon which branch of the socioeconomic tree you perch. But one fact is indisputable: traditional print media—especially magazine and book publishing—is on the decline. Amazon recently announced that it sold more ebooks than either hardcover books or paperback books. Prediction: By the time the second edition of this book is published, ebook sales will exceed hardcover and paperback sales combined.

All this means employment opportunities in traditional print media are on the decline as well. Today, college grads with journalism degrees can't find work. Writers and editors in bricks-and-mortar publishing are being laid off in record numbers, and in most cases the companies have no intention of ever rehiring or replacing them.

Meanwhile, thanks to Smartphones and other wireless devices, online magazines and newspapers are ever more accessible. Media companies that previously gave away online content for free are searching for ways to create revenue streams. The *New York Times* recently announced a campaign to expand its online presence, including a plan to charge for different access levels. The company already has two hundred employees working in the online division.

The stars are in alignment. This is the perfect time for entrepreneurs to set up shop on the Internet. Remember, though, if you're going to be an entrepreneur, you must think like one. Besides considering the approaches presented in this book, let your mind roam free until it latches onto an idea with "potential." Maybe nobody's ever done it before; maybe it's been done but you can do it better; or maybe the marketplace has room for yet another voice, your voice. Of course, you may not succeed. But one thing is certain: you won't succeed if you do nothing.

Blake is not a do-nothing kind of guy. The entrepreneur of the team, he recently took an idea from concept to fruition in the compressed time frame encouraged by the Internet. Seeing a need and trying to fill it, he has launched a new site, mediadesignpublishing.com, to help writers convert their manuscripts to Kindle and Nook formats. Success or failure is not predictable, but this is: Win, lose, or draw, Blake will put another idea into play soon.

The trend toward the Internet's dominance of the media is as inexorable as an avalanche. The question is, are you going to ride the crest—or be buried?

Ebook Editing and Conversion Services

eBook Conversion

Do you have an irrepressible urge to convert your electronic manuscript into an eBook?

We can help!

We do eBook Conversion to Amazon Kindle and Barnes & Noble Nook formats, for both individual authors and publishers.

Converting a document into an eBook requires manual editing and formatting to make it function properly and look good in Amazon Kindle, Barnes & Noble Nook, and other hand-held devices. Improper formatting can result in book returns and bad reviews.

We prepare and format titles to be viewer friendly on all devices.

eBook Editing

Before You Submit Your Manuscript . . . make it as good as possible.

Every writer needs to be edited. Every manuscript will benefit from a fresh pair of eyes, a critical mind, a professional editor's scalpel. That's what we offer.

Whether you're pursuing eBook publishing, traditional publishing or Print on Demand, you'll have to live with what goes between the covers of your book for many years. Do you really want to publish something that makes you wince every time you pass the bookshelf?

Send your work to us for a Free Manuscript Evaluation—and improve its marketability.
After evaluating your submission, one of our editors will offer detailed feedback and recommendations.

http://www.mediadesignpublishing.com/contact/

To learn more, contact:

Media Design Services, Inc.
P.O. Box 3153
Santa Rosa, CA 95402

blake@mediadesign-mds.com

707-836-8389